Amazing Snakes OF THE Northwest

Parker Holmes

PowerKiDS press
New York

Published in 2015 by The Rosen Publishing Group, Inc.
29 East 21st Street, New York, NY 10010

First Edition

Editor: Jennifer Way
Book Design: Andrew Povolny
Photo Research: Katie Stryker

Photo Credits: Cover, pp. 9, 10, 16 Jared Hobbs/All Canada Photos/Getty Images; pp. 5, 18, 21 (bottom), 22 (top), 22 (middle) James Gerholdt/Photolibrary/Getty Images; p. 6 R. Andrew Odum/Photolibrary/Getty Images; p. 7 Chris Mattison/age fotostock/Getty Images; p. 12 Joe McDonald/Visuals Unlimited, Inc./Getty Images; p. 13 Frank Lukasseck/Photolibrary/Getty Images; p. 15 Stuart Wilson/Photo Researchers/Getty Images; p. 19 Bill Gorum/Flickr Open/Getty Images; p. 20 John Serrao/Photo Researchers/Getty Images; p. 21 (top) Jim Merli/Visuals Unlimited/Getty Images; p. 22 Danita Delimont/Gallo Images/Getty Images.

Library of Congress Cataloging-in-Publication Data

Holmes, Parker, author.
Amazing snakes of the Northwest / by Parker Holmes. — First edition.
pages cm. — (Amazing snakes)
Includes index.
ISBN 978-1-4777-6507-4 (library binding) — ISBN 978-1-4777-6508-1 (pbk.) — ISBN 978-1-4777-6509-8 (6-pack)
1. Snakes—Northwestern States–Juvenile literature. I. Title.
QL666.O6H753 2015
597.96'0979—dc23
2013044857

Manufactured in the United States of America

CPSIA Compliance Information: Batch #WS14PK6: For Further Information contact Rosen Publishing, New York, New York at 1-800-237-9932

Contents

Snakes of All Sizes	4
Rubber Boa	6
Western Yellow-Bellied Racer	8
Sharp-Tailed Snake	10
Western Rattlesnake	12
Desert Striped Whipsnake	14
Northwestern Garter Snake	16
Gopher Snake	18
Seeing Snakes	20
Other Snakes in the Northwest	22
Glossary	23
Index	24
Websites	24

Snakes of All Sizes

Do you like to find snakes? In the Northwest, you can find some very interesting kinds. You might come across a giant gopher snake that's 6 feet (2 m) long. Or you might see a sharp-tailed snake that's less than 1 foot (30 cm) long. You could spot a snake, such as the yellow-bellied racer, climbing up a tree. Or you could find one, such as the ringneck snake, hiding under a rock. Snakes in the Northwest come in all sizes, and they live in all kinds of **habitats**. Close to 20 **species** live in this **region**.

Most snakes in the Northwest aren't dangerous. There's only one kind of **venomous** snake here—the western rattlesnake. Be careful! Venomous snakes are what many people call poisonous snakes. But if you're looking for snakes in this area, you're more likely to come across a harmless kind. Let's take a look at some exciting snakes of the Northwest!

The striped whipsnake is found from central Washington south to Mexico.

Rubber Boa

When you first look at a rubber boa, you might have trouble telling its head from its tail. Some people call these snakes two-headed snakes because their heads and thick tails are almost the same size. These harmless **reptiles** are related to the giant boa **constrictors** of Latin America. But rubber boas are only about 1.5 to 2 feet (46–61 cm) long. They're shy little snakes that like to hide under logs and rocks. Rubber boas are very gentle and almost never bite people. If threatened, a rubber boa will often curl into a ball and hide its head.

Rubber boas are constrictors, which means that they wrap themselves around their food and squeeze it to death. They eat mostly small **mammals**, such as baby mice. Can you guess why these snakes are called rubber boas? It is because their smooth brown skin looks and feels like rubber.

Here you can see how shiny and rubbery the rubber boa's skin looks. It is found in each of the northwestern states.

Rubber boas are usually tan or brown, but they can also be yellow, orange, or olive green.

Western Yellow-Bellied Racer

Racer snakes are built for action! These long, slender snakes can move really fast, and they're excellent climbers. They're the natural athletes of the snake world. There are several types of racer snakes throughout the country, and the western yellow-bellied racer is one found in the Northwest. There are two types of yellow-bellied racers here—the eastern and western kinds. These snakes are dark colored but have yellow bellies. They usually grow to about 3 to 4 feet (.9–1.2 m). These snakes are not picky eaters. They'll eat just about anything they can find, including insects, lizards, frogs, birds, and mice. They'll sometimes climb into bushes and trees looking for meals.

Racer snakes don't make good pets. They're **feisty** snakes that will probably bite if you pick them up. If they feel threatened, they might also **vibrate** their tails against the ground, sounding kind of like a rattlesnake.

The western yellow-bellied racer lives in Oregon, Washington, Idaho, and Montana in the Northwest.

Sharp-Tailed Snake

Sharp-tailed snakes can use their pointy tales as a defense.

It's not easy to find a sharp-tailed snake. These secretive little snakes are very good at hiding. During the day, they spend most of their time hiding under rocks or logs or sometimes underground. They usually come out only at night. If you do see one, at first you might think it's just a big worm. These harmless snakes normally grow to only between 8 and 12 inches (20–30 cm), and they're often not any thicker than a pencil. They usually look gray or brown. Can you guess why they're called sharp-tailed snakes? You guessed it—their tails are very sharp and pointed at the end.

These snakes never have to ask, "What's for dinner?" It's always the same thing—slugs. That's about all they eat. Sharp-tailed snakes are well adapted to eat these slimy creatures. They have long teeth that help them hold on to the slippery slugs.

Western Rattlesnake

The northern Pacific rattlesnake, shown here, is a western rattlesnake found in the Northwest.

There's only one kind of snake in the Northwest that you want to avoid—the western rattlesnake. It's the only venomous snake in the region. Lucky for us, though, rattlesnakes usually warn us if we're getting too close. These snakes will shake the rattles on their tails. That's their way of saying, "Please go away!" Remember that rattlesnakes aren't looking for a fight. They just want to be left alone.

There are three varieties of western rattlesnakes mainly seen here: the northern Pacific, the Great Basin, and the prairie rattlesnake. These snakes usually grow to 3 to 4 feet (.9–1.2 m), sometimes larger. They're often brown with darker blotches. Western rattlesnakes like to hunt for small mammals, such as squirrels, mice, and rabbits. They use their sharp fangs and deadly venom to kill the food. This venom can also be dangerous to humans. So always be careful if you hear that rattling sound—bzzzz!

The prairie rattlesnake is a western rattlesnake that is generally found from just east of the Rocky Mountains to the Great Plains.

Desert Striped Whipsnake

If you see a snake that's as skinny as a whip, you might actually be looking at a snake called a whipsnake. There are several types of whipsnakes in the country, and the one that lives in this region is called the desert striped whipsnake. This **subspecies** is found from the Southwest all the way to the Northwest. It's a long, skinny snake that grows to about 4 feet (1.2 m), sometimes longer. These snakes usually have dark bodies with light stripes.

Whipsnakes are related to the group of snakes called racers. That means they can move really fast. This speed helps them catch their next meal. Whipsnakes will eat all kinds of food, including lizards, insects, small birds, and even other snakes. Whipsnakes have good eyesight, and they like to slither around hunting for food with their heads raised high above the ground. If you're a lizard, you better watch out!

In the Northwest, whipsnakes may seek shelter in trees.

Northwestern Garter Snake

The northwestern garter snake is found in Oregon and Washington in the Northwest.

If you're looking for snakes in the Northwest, the garter snake might be the first snake you find. Garter snakes are one of the most common snakes in the region. They're also one of the most common snakes in the entire country. Many people mistakenly call them garden snakes, but they're actually garter snakes. There are many species of garter snakes in the United States, and the northwestern garter is one type that lives here.

The northwestern garter likes to live near the edges of forests or in fields. That's where these snakes can find their favorite food—slugs and earthworms. Sometimes you'll find the snakes hiding under boards or logs. They grow to about 2 feet (61 cm) long, and they usually have dark bodies with colored stripes. Garter snakes are harmless, but they may bite if you pick them up. They also might squirt you with stinky **musk** and poop. Yuck!

Gopher Snake

Sssss! That's the hissing sound that gopher snakes like to make. They're one of the loudest hissers in the snake world. They're also one of the biggest snakes in the Northwest. If you see one, it may coil up and hiss. It may even vibrate its tail against the ground, sounding like a rattlesnake. But don't worry. Gopher snakes may act scary, but they're really harmless.

The bull snake, shown here, is a subspecies of the gopher snake. This bull snake is eating a chipmunk.

This gopher snake is coiled and hissing, showing that it is ready to defend itself from an enemy.

There are three types of gopher snakes in the Northwest—the Pacific gopher, Great Basin gopher, and the bull snake. These snakes often grow to 4 to 5 feet (1.2–1.5 m) and can be bigger. The longest bull snake ever recorded was 8.5 feet (2.6 m)! Gopher snakes are constrictors and like to eat **rodents**, such as gophers, rats, and mice. They sometimes hang out in animal **burrows**, such as gopher holes, to find food and rest. They have various colors, often with dark blotches, and people sometimes think they look like rattlesnakes.

Seeing Snakes

You can find some exciting snakes in the Northwest. But you won't see quite as many kinds here as you would in warmer places. The Northwest gets cold, and snakes don't like chilly weather. Snakes are cold-blooded. That means they need warm weather to keep their bodies at the most comfortable temperature. Because of that, not quite as many species live in this region.

The green snake, or grass snake, is a harmless snake that is found in North America.

Ringneck snakes are dark on top but have colorful underbellies and rings around their necks.

You won't see the snakes that do live here all the time either. They **hibernate** and often disappear during the winter.

Are you scared of snakes? If so, remember that most snakes here aren't dangerous. You're most likely to run into a harmless kind, such as a garter, racer, ringneck, gopher, or green snake. Remember, too, that snakes are **beneficial** because they eat lots of insects and rodents. Snakes are fascinating creatures. Wouldn't you like to see one? The Northwest has some great snakes!

Garter snakes are the most widespread kind of snake found in North America.

Other Snakes in the Northwest

- California mountain king snake
- Common garter snake
- Desert night snake
- Ground snake
- Pale milk snake
- Plains garter snake
- Plains hognose
- Ringneck snake
- Smooth green snake
- Western terrestrial garter snake

Smooth green snake

Plains hognose snake

California mountain king snake

Glossary

beneficial (beh-nuh-FIH-shul) Helpful, producing good.

burrows (BUR-ohz) Holes animals dig in the ground.

constrictors (kun-STRIKT-urz) Snakes that kill by wrapping their bodies around their prey and squeezing.

feisty (FY-stee) Quick to fight or show aggression.

habitats (HA-buh-tats) The surroundings where animals or plants naturally live.

hibernate (HY-bur-nayt) To spend the winter in a sleeplike state.

mammals (MA-mulz) Warm-blooded animals that have backbones and hair, breathe air, and feed milk to their young.

musk (MUSK) Strong-smelling matter given off by an animal's body.

region (REE-jun) One of the different parts of Earth.

reptiles (REP-tylz) Cold-blooded animals with lungs and scales.

rodents (ROH-dents) Animals with gnawing teeth, such as mice.

species (SPEE-sheez) A single kind of living thing. All people are one species.

subspecies (SUB-spee-sheez) Types within a species.

venomous (VEH-nuh-mis) Having a poisonous bite.

vibrate (VY-brayt) To move back and forth quickly.

Index

B
bellies, 8

C
constrictors, 6, 19

F
food, 6, 13–14, 17, 19

I
insects, 8, 14, 21

L
logs, 6, 11, 17

M
mammals, 6, 13
mice, 6, 8, 13, 19

R
region, 4, 12, 14, 17, 20
reptiles, 6
rock(s), 4, 6, 11
rodents, 19, 21

S
skin, 6
species, 4, 17, 20
subspecies, 14

T
tail(s), 6, 8, 11–12, 18

V
venom, 13

W
western rattlesnake(s), 4, 12–13

Y
yellow-bellied racer(s), 4, 8

Websites

Due to the changing nature of Internet links, PowerKids Press has developed an online list of websites related to the subject of this book. This site is updated regularly. Please use this link to access the list:
www.powerkidslinks.com/amaz/nwes/